Spiritual Awakening
(the easy way)

HAY HOUSE

Carlsbad, California • New York City • London • Sydney
Johannesburg • Vancouver • Hong Kong • New Delhi

To Sammy
(My teacher and the neighbour's dog)

First published and distributed in the United Kingdom by:
Hay House UK Ltd, Astley House, 33 Notting Hill Gate, London W11 3JQ
Tel: +44 (0)20 3675 2450 • Fax: +44 (0)20 3675 2451 • www.hayhouse.co.uk

Published and distributed in the United States of America by:
Hay House Inc., PO Box 5100, Carlsbad, CA 92018-5100
Tel: (1) 760 431 7695 or (800) 654 5126 • Fax: (1) 760 431 6948 or (800) 650 5115
www.hayhouse.com

Published and distributed in Australia by:
Hay House Australia Ltd, 18/36 Ralph St, Alexandria NSW 2015
Tel: (61) 2 9669 4299 • Fax: (61) 2 9669 4144 • www.hayhouse.com.au

Published and distributed in the Republic of South Africa by:
Hay House SA (Pty) Ltd, PO Box 990, Witkoppen 2068
Tel/Fax: (27) 11 467 8904 • www.hayhouse.co.za

Published and distributed in India by:
Hay House Publishers India, Muskaan Complex, Plot No.3, B-2, Vasant Kunj,
New Delhi 110 070 • Tel: (91) 11 4176 1620 • Fax: (91) 11 4176 1630
www.hayhouse.co.in

Distributed in Canada by:
Raincoast, 9050 Shaughnessy St, Vancouver BC V6P 6E5
Tel: (1) 604 323 7100 • Fax: (1) 604 323 2600

Text © Tim van der Vliet, 2013
www.timvandervliet.com

The moral rights of the author have been asserted.

Cover and book design by www.designtree.nl
Edited by www.theglobalwriter.com and www.juliawillard.com

A catalogue record for this book is available from the British Library.

Readers of This Book

If you read this book and decide to pass it along to someone else, please add your details in the space below to show the path this book travels:

Name	Country
_____	_____
_____	_____
_____	_____
_____	_____
_____	_____
_____	_____
_____	_____
_____	_____
_____	_____
_____	_____
_____	_____

Name   **Country**

_____   _____

_____   _____

_____   _____

_____   _____

_____   _____

_____   _____

_____   _____

_____   _____

_____   _____

_____   _____

Table of contents

14   Break free

28   Let go

56   Have fun

66   Feel the Force

82   Move towards the light

Introduction

In life we all have the same goal: to seek our greatest joy. We have the natural ability and innate desire to move towards our joy and away from our pain, yet this is often forgotten. People use different names for the process of finding joy, such as 'spiritual awakening' and 'enlightenment'. Sometimes the idea of enlightenment is offputting due to its seeming obsurity and also because so few people have found an enlightened path. It is in fact easier than most people find it to be, which may be the difficult thing about it. We are all born enlightened. All we have to do is forget what we have learned and go back to our natural, enlightened state. *Spiritual Awakening (the easy way)* is about this process, which starts with the will to change and to see clearly. It's just a decision.

On my path, inspired by daily experiences, the people around me and information that came to me, I had some insights and thoughts that I am sharing with you in this book. Though each of these insights stand alone, I've put them into a construct of five chapters or steps. The first step is to break free from our collective dream. The second step is to detach and to let go of our beliefs. Step three reminds us to have fun along the way. Step four observes the way things start to change in life, for at this stage we start to experience a kind of flow or Force (just like in the *Star Wars* movies). Finally, step five, the final stage of the journey, discusses how we can move towards the light.

Hopefully you will take these thoughts with you in your daily life, and have a bit of fun doing so.

Tim van der Vliet | Tim Facebook ➟ Tim van der Vliet
                           Tim Twitter ➟ @Tim2day

Enlightenment brought me absolutely nothing

- Buddha -

Bre

ak

free

I try to forget
about the good and the bad
or worse and better
Then the heart of the matter
in daily life is:
fewer obligations
are just so much better.

If Gandhi could see that change is the only constant in this world,

who are we to disagree?

Walk in my shoes
for a month
before you tell me
what you think.

Be in sync before
you label me
and put your
unwritten rules
all over me.
Just walk in my
shoes before
you judge me.

I am taught
to be critical
especially of me
I see now
that I do the negative mantra
I cannot I cannot I cannot
This mantra holds me down
But I want to fly
so I replace it with
I can I can I can
For each negative thought
that comes to mind
I turn it around
I say three times
thank you thank you thank you
for everything that is as it is.

Here I find
myself suddenly
with a positive state of mind
And my daily path
becomes of another
but much lighter kind.

Don't just agree with everything you see
Make a difference
You can change the world
change life
by changing yourself
There is always a choice
There is always a choice
There is always a choice
Repeat this mantra when you're in trouble
or bored.

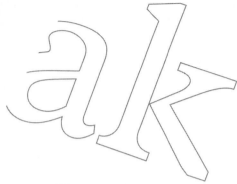

I forget the rules
'cause the only thing that really rules
is the love that uncurls in my world
You want to be with the boyz that hate?
Fine
but remember that their mind state
is also a choice.

Check: are there a lot of people around
you that hate? If you can't take it, get out.

Just a thought
on gurus and
their followers...

Would Jesus have been a Christian?
Muhammad a Muslim?
Buddha a Buddhist?
Of course not!
The only thing they claim
is that you should follow your own aim
As far as they're concerned
there's no such thing
as a guru,
'cause the only guru
is
you.
So don't follow
if you want to be in the flow
You are the only one
in your life show
Now you know
be a rebel
go and find your truth
and forget those people
(like me)
who tell you how to.

**In my quest
for eternal youth**

**in
search
for
truth**

I found one thing:
truth is based on opinion
on what the average idiot thinks
believes to be true
Truth itself simply doesn't exist
So when fighting my walls
built by years of education
with every step I make
from the shelf of my truth library
a brick I take
I see that with each truth
I am facing myself
the average idiot part in me
That makes me smile
I take the wall down in laughter
and find thereafter
that truth
is inside me.

Whenever you hear the word God, replace it with the word Life. Immediately you'll see who is fooling you and who is not.

Exercise

Let go

What is black?
They say that all colours
from infrared to violet
come together in white
And true
white is beautiful
but why is black so Black?
I love black!
Black cars
black clothes
black shades
Even my so-called black side I embrace
and hence I face
all the stuff I didn't want to see
With that the light shines through
all of these black dreams
on to me
The picture is complete.

black IS SO beautiful

Identity is never static
So if you know it's going to change
why take it seriously?
Lose the image
let go of that ego
feel the dynamics
and start surfing.

Check

With what do you identify yourself?
Is it your car, clothes, girls?
Is that really what life is about?

All we want to do is rise, rise into a next stage, a better atmosphere

It's easier if your heart is clear
So ask yourself in all you do
Is this based on love or fear
The fearless may have
an unusual point of view
which might seem funny
but without despair
the road of life is way more sunny

You just have to dare.

The most nasty person on my way
I try to see as a teacher today
I bless and bless and try to see
the good thing in the man in front of me
because he too was born an innocent baby
Bless your biggest enemy
your boss, neighbour
whoever it may be
The nastiness
turns around
It shifts to a higher ground
of consciousness

Exercise

Do this every day.

Though we aim for perfection
which means to educate and teach
perfection remains
hard to reach.

The black diamond of fear
is to be a nobody
to live an empty life
not having a self
or too much of one
I too fear
that I'm not completing it yet
as I'm supposed to
By recognizing this
I jump off the cliff
into the black river
and swimming there in confusion
I see
that my fear
was just another illusion.

If it's an illusion why is it so real?

This is because people, us
him me she or we
think it's real
That thought pattern creates a vibe
an energy so to speak
By following that grid of energy
the dream becomes stronger
There is no better or wrong
but when you break free
you just feel like going on
You see
that you can use the illusion
for you
to form
a better me.

Check

Do you agree that fear is based on an illusion?

Every thought of fear
is based on duality
that there are 'the Others'
pointing the finger –
you against me.

The truth is
there is only one Unity
there is only we,
we humanity
or we the Universe
Dualism is an illusion.

Sleepless nights are often the beginning of a (very) positive change

the ☼ side of life

The confusion of an illusion
is a spiritual matter
Something in the trinity of body mind and spirit
is not perfectly aligned
and that
in fact
is the mind.
In condition of past and future
it believes
the newspapers to be true

Be out of mind

and you'll find this dream popping
as a big blue balloon on a sunny day does
This is your birth
eyes are open
wipe out the sleep
be meek
and you will inherit the Earth.

I feel a chill
from tail to crown
no thoughts
total relaxation
My experience is now
and real
Total escape from Earthly reality
dependencies
and other non-necessities
I breathe out
Relieved, I try to stand
I flush
and wash my hands.

There is the rat race

there is the human race

Where are you?

Patriarchy

look around
it's what you see

It's a society
based on
money
money
money...

Fellow man
it's time
to leave the battlefield
and let mama matriarchy
explore her possibilities
It's time for space in our hearts
instead of the illusions we embrace
It's time to contemplate
It's time for flowers in the battlefield
It's time to give her the key
and to wait
and see

Women (and men!)
It really is time to let this heart energy of yours rule.

Space

...is good

Letting fly
Letting go

True love
is also facing

what we really can...

...Is it hard to let go?
It does seem so
but letting go
to detach
is all we should know
I mean in the rise
and in the fall
in essence it's just a ride
Don't hide
enjoy!
There are angels on your side
No boundaries is what should be deployed
so you can graduate to the high life.

There is no better way
Better is a myth
There is only different

have
fun

I got this
insight from
a Tibetan monk
Simply bright
and so true
and strong…

This is what he said:

"It's really simple:
the goal in life
is to be happy
And happiness
is all in the mind you know
Taming the mind
that what people find so hard to find
is basically
to chill out
to relax,
Chillax!"

After that
he laughed his special Tibetan laugh
It starts with a grin
and ends in the belly
I laugh with him
'cause I like this way of thinking.

Never forget
Never
Forget
Rule number

6

It's enlightening
a bit frightening
With this cutting edge knowledge
the knowledge of rule number 6
you are still in a moment
of total consciousness
What bliss!
Rule number 6
Feels mighty and so free
Rule number 6 is:
STOP taking yourself so bloody seriously.

Other rules
don't really
exist.

God is
of course ALL
but have you
ever realized
that God
spelled backwards
is DOG?

Makes you think doesn't it?

And when I do think of it
a dog is exactly
how we would want to be:
faithful
in peace
no memories of the past
no worries about the future
running after bikes
enthusiastic for no reason
and pissing everywhere you like

God, what a lesson!
So now for my spiritual lesson
'cause I always want more
I go to **Sammy**
the Dog of the girl next door.

Pure Happiness

Feel
th
Forc

They say

mind over matter
money on your mind
mind on your money

But I find that
when I focus on alternative energies
it becomes spirit over mind over matter
If spirit's over mind
the core is strong
and all these mind and matter things
just come along.

My path
known to Him
is in my system
in my cells
like little spells
being cast
one by one
as pieces
of the puzzle
of my path.

The mind creates words
words are a filter
they distort

By not talking about a fact
you keep it simple
you keep it pure

The magic
is
still
intact

Every thought we have
every word we speak
every action we take
All we do has an effect
Even the smallest thing
is influencing
the Universe
Like every wave hits the coast
If we understand our bodies
feel no shame of what we became
we understand the Universe
because everywhere is happening
exactly the same.

The truth is in here.

Check

Can you feel it?

simple *is* pure
pure *is* simple
That simple?
Yes.

However
everybody wants to be pure
but nobody wants to be simple
This is the great misunderstanding
the illusion
we humans are in
Be simple
be pure
Feel this truth
Look at a Japanese garden
or how stupid you get
when drinking with friends...

The blessing of emptiness
is the art of happiness
An empty mind
is a simple mind
Be simple and find
your heart pure
and your life in the divine.

The air on which I float
contains all information
I should know
All the ways
that I can follow
The breeze on which I slide
makes me collide
with everything happening
The tornado on which I roll
I enjoy
The ride accelerates
I feel the bungee and touch the sky
Here I dive
but it's OK
because I know for every low
there is a high
In the centre
say the zero point
there's nothing else but stillness
Satisfied
with all the flights,

I land
I smile
and see
the light

The essence in 4 words

no mind
no problem

The message is clear
It comes from right above
Then comes the mind
It makes words
It filters the divine
The soul message
the thing that makes you feel fine
appears in between the lines.

We are water molecules in the river called

Earth

The mirror hypnosis

**Look straight into
your right eye
and smile
Breathe three times
slow and deep
to the belly
1…
2…
3…
Now what you see
is your new true *me*.**

Exercise

Do this every time you see a mirror. Maybe check if you are alone first so you don't look too much like a fool.

If the status quo is in sight
it's time to go
For me unchanged
is a joke
The dream I am in
doesn't always match the perfect life,
the illusion of 'keep things as they are'
I hear a voice, it says:
further is the way
I leave everything behind
and find myself
in an untangled state of mind
I realize that I
put the *me* in me
the guy that writes this poetry
without mercy
to work for my heart,
my higher me
This is the moment
the flow is felt
as a golden stream
And then the Universe-ty says:

Hey!
This guy is living in non-duality
He is ready for the lessons of Unity
And on my path
the light shines bright.

A thought:
Unchanged doesn't really exist
You don't want to keep things as they are.

Move towards the light

What is enlightenment?
Seeing the light
Sometimes I feel it's far away
as a distant bright light
almost out of sight
But other times
there is focus in mind
I close my eyes
and a smile arises
Then I see the light
the essence of what is
The meaning of it *all*
= *one*, not *two*
and it's not in the future
nor in the past
but right now and here
behind these closed eyes.

The only rule
is no rule
as in none
is ALL
or all
is ONE.

we are symbiotic
a piece of the same
puzzle so intrinsic
we are all the same
all we are

all

Every moment
every time
is perfect
It is the only thing that is
And what is, is

A thought:
If there is really only one thing
and therefore no reference point
can it be anything other than perfect?

In my sleep
I fly
to this other planet
this city of light
where love rules
and sentient beings remain
And you
are there too
It is true
that in the end
we're all the same
In our dreams
we meet again
Together we fly
In the morning
we wake up from the light
with new divine insights
The start of a new day
grateful for this way.

Light is life
Life is God
All life grows
from the colours red to violet
That is the spectrum
we can see
The light travels
with light speed
With light comes love
that we all seek

Note:
When you break down molecules into particles
it breaks down to mostly photons
photons = light

We *are* light
even in the scientific form
We just have to remember this.

Let's forget about enlightenment
and start enlightening

Let's forget about healing
and be healed

Don't listen to all of this
Feel your core
Go and explore
yourself
Find out more…

To be

continued...

Please use this space in a creative way...

About the author

Tim van der Vliet cut his teeth in the financial markets, where he spent 13 years trading stock, forex, futures and options. There, in the place he least expected it, he learned one of his first life lessons: a good trader must be fully present, and have neither ego nor memory. No ego because a trader who operates from fear, or who is too confident, makes mistakes. No memory because what matters is not the past but the trade of the moment. After 13 years, he bade goodbye to that world to write about the things are closer to his heart... more about life and the human race. Tim lives in Amsterdam with his wife and children. He spends as much time as possible sitting in front of his house doing nothing, so to create space and time to be creative.

Inspired by

Ghandi
Milan Hofmans (Project M)
Jesus, Buddha and Muhammad
Messenger Mini-Books
Neale Donald Walsch
Lost (the series)
India.Arie
Steve the neighbour
Wyclef Jean
Jay-Z and Alicia Keys
Lama Lobsang
An anonymous English prime minister
Sammy (pseudonym for Arie, the neighbour's bulldog)
A blank page
Obi-Wan Kenobi
Silence (inside and outside)
The Pacific Ocean
Bob (at 6AM in ING bar in Kyoto, Japan)
Earth, Sun, the Moon and the Universe
The bathroom and myself in the mirror
Jed McKenna
Thea Terlouw
My colleagues at Source
Amsterdam and her beautiful people.

Gratitude to

Unom for your initial spark, Po for truly getting me started, Nicole for your presence and soulmateness, Dorien for your creative flow, Renata and Julia for your right on time words, Gee for your ever-positive energy, Kris and Tijn for your unlimited faith (and roof sessions), Sammy for your spiritual lessons, Rick for taking this further, Miho, Yuan, Rio, Lila and Liam for this life show. Atalwin and Rik for last moment additions, Ellen for design tips, Mom for making me and my (lack of) education, Steve for insights at Karma Corner, Yvez for last-minute design, Chris and Marijme for your words and the life you bring, Didu for an unexpected smile, Marc for putting in a mindful view, Verena for your vision, and all the people I connect with in this world...

Thank you!

Check out www.TimvanderVliet.com for more material and inspiration from Tim van der Vliet.

10% of the royalties from this book are donated to charity. See the Author/Charity section on the website for more info.

Does *Spiritual Awakening (the easy way)* inspire you to start waking up yourself? Visit the get for free section on timvandervliet.com and subscribe to Tim's *13 Steps to Spiritual Awakening (the easy way)*.

13 Steps to Spiritual Awakening (the easy way) is a practical mini-course that complements the book. It consists of real life examples and easy-to-do exercises that help you break free from worrying. It's easy and for free! Each step will be sent to your mailbox on a weekly basis. So visit the get for free section on timvandervliet.com and start living joyfully from the heart. The easy way!

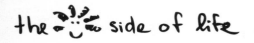

I like to see the future according to me
may seem like a dream for some
but it's what is happening around me
and it looks like it started inside me

In essence humanity is just one organism
a collective energy
With that in mind there is no more me
there is only we, we humanity

Now, whatever you give away to your other me
your sister or brother
You know how it goes
What comes around goes around

Start with giving away the stuff that you don't need
It could be clothes, it could be cars
And don't think,
"What did that just cost me?"

Give away with a smile
Giving away is the art of pleasure
You'll find the current to ride
open doors to explore

This is the evolution of Give
the Givolution
We give away the constitution
and order the Give Away Revolution.

Follow Tim on Twitter @Tim2Day
or get connected to the Facebook Tim van der Vliet.

Pass this book along. Start giving away.
Feel the Force. Be the change.

make a choice
make a change.